CHILDREN'S ILLUSTRATED
ENCYCLOPEDIA

ALLIGATOR

Contents

© 2005 Alligator Books Ltd
Published by Alligator Books Ltd
Gadd House, Arcadia Avenue
London N3 2JU

Edited by Virginia Kerley
and Alexia Horner
Printed in China
ISBN-10: 1-84239-491-6
ISBN-13: 978-1-84239-491-5

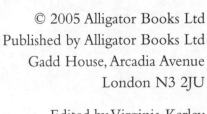

THE UNIVERSE

On a clear night, the human eye can see around 3,000 stars in the sky

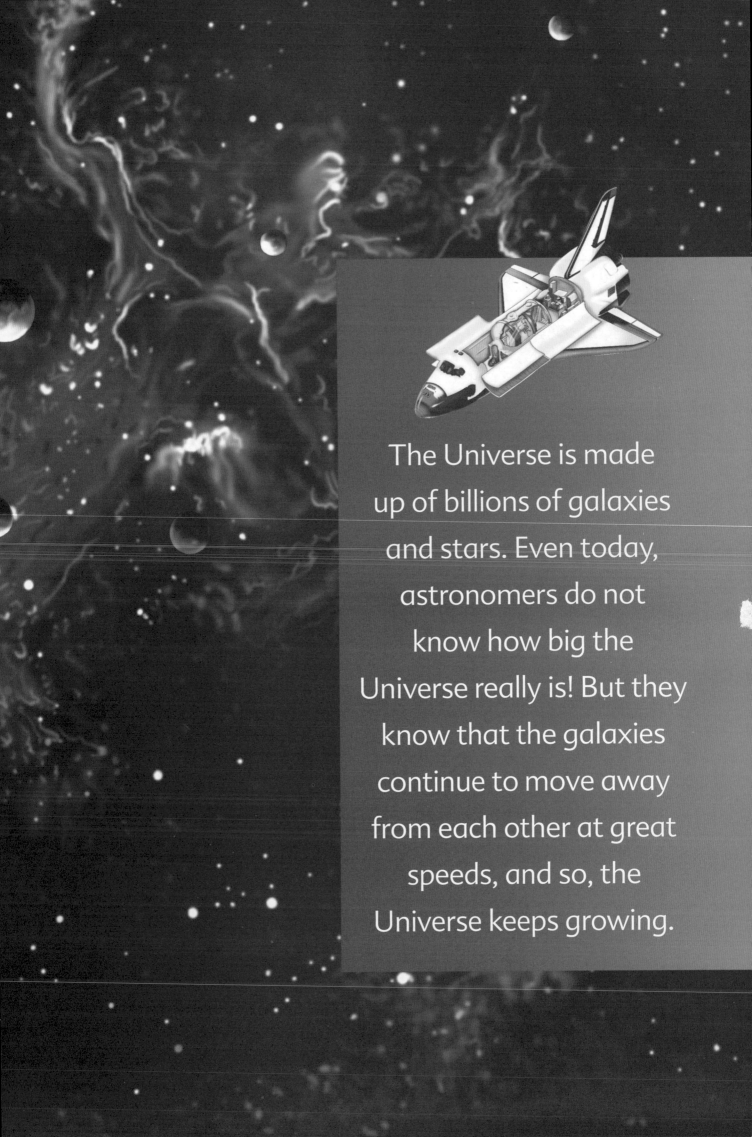

The Universe is made up of billions of galaxies and stars. Even today, astronomers do not know how big the Universe really is! But they know that the galaxies continue to move away from each other at great speeds, and so, the Universe keeps growing.

Galaxies and Stars

Galaxies are massive collections of stars, gas and dust. They are found in various shapes and sizes. A star is born from a combination of gas and dust. When the gases burn themselves out, the star dies. A star may live for several million years.

Types of Galaxies

Spiral Galaxies: These galaxies have long twisting arms and give birth to new stars. Some of these new stars are very large and bright. Our galaxy, the Milky Way, is a spiral galaxy.

The spirals that we see around galaxies are dust clouds lit up by stars near them!

Believe me!!!

Galaxies crash into one another. However, no damage occurs during these accidents. Many galaxies have passed right through our own Milky Way!

Elliptical Galaxies: Most of these galaxies are egg shaped and do not have spiral arms. Elliptical galaxies have very little gas or dust, and do not give birth to new stars.

Irregular Galaxies: These galaxies do not have a regular shape and are made up of gas, dust and a few new stars.

Asteroids are space rocks that move around the Sun.

Types of Stars

Red Dwarf: These stars are smaller than the sun and live for trillions of years. They are not as hot as most other stars.

Yellow Star: Like our Sun, these stars live for about 10 billion years. Towards the end of their life, they swell up before shrinking again.

Blue Giant: These have a short life and live for only 10,000 – 100,000 years. Blue Giants are very hot.

Supernovas:
The giant stars end their lives in a massive explosion called the supernova. When a star explodes, it shines brightly for a long time.

Orion:
Popularly known as The Hunter, this constellation has many names. It is called the Giant in Syria and the Sahu in Egypt.

Constellations

A specific pattern of stars is called a constellation. Most constellations have Greek names.

Ursa Major: This is the oldest constellation and is made up of seven stars. It is also known as the Great Bear and the Big Dipper. According to legend, the constellation depicts the story of hunters in pursuit of a bear.

Ursa Minor: This constellation is shaped like a bent spoon, and is known as the Little Bear or the Little Dipper. According to Greek mythology, Ursa Minor is the son of Ursa Major, and they follow each other through the galaxy.

Most asteroids lie in the Asteroid Belt, between Mars and Jupiter.

Solar System and the Planets

Our Solar System is huge. The Sun is the central force of the Solar System. Moving around the Sun are nine planets, their moons and several comets and asteroids.

Sun: The Sun is in fact, a huge star. It is so huge that you could fit a million Earths into it!

Mercury: It is the closest planet to the Sun. You would weigh less than half your weight on this planet! Why? Because, the gravity on Mercury is less than that on Earth. Mercury does not have a moon.

Venus: Like Earth, Venus also has volcanoes, valleys and mountains, but it is very hot. Venus, too, has no moon.

The Earth has one moon named Luna, which moves around it the same way that the Earth moves around the Sun. Luna is made of solid rock, and has mountains, valleys, volcanoes and many deep holes called craters.

Saturn

Mars

Jupiter

Earth

Venus

Mercury

Sun

Earth: We live on this planet. It is the only planet known to support life.

Mars: It is also known as the Red Planet. Scientists believe that water bodies like rivers, lakes and oceans once existed here. Mars has two moons - Deimos and Phobos.

Jupiter: The Solar System's largest planet is made up of huge amounts of gas and liquids. It has 61 moons, more than any other planet!

Saturn: This planet is made of gases and liquids. It is easily recognised because of its beautiful rings. Saturn has 31 moons.

Uranus: This planet is made up of clouds and has a rocky centre. Uranus seems to lie on its side.

Comets are made up of ice and rocky dust. They are not very large and move around the Sun. The most famous comet is Halley's Comet. It takes 76 years to go around the Sun.

Pluto

Neptune

nus

Neptune: It is one of the farthest planets in the Solar System. This planet is made of gaseous clouds and has six rings around it. Neptune has 13 known moons.

Pluto: According to Roman legend, Pluto is believed to be the God of the Underworld. It is the smallest planet and has only one moon, called Charon.

Word Wizard

Satellite: Natural or man-made objects that move around another space body are called satellites. The moon is a natural satellite, but man has also sent some artificial satellites into space.

Saturn has 31 moons.

Man and Outer Space

"Three, two, one…blast off!" Space exploration has always fascinated Man. A number of rockets and shuttles have been sent into space to explore what lies beyond. Some carry a team of astronauts on board while others are sent unmanned to collect information and rock samples.

Yuri Gagarin was the first man to travel into space, on a spaceship called Vostok 1.

Mission to Space

Manned missions are spacecraft that carry astronauts into space. Space Shuttle Vostok 1 was the first manned mission and was sent into space on 12 April, 1961. A shuttle orbiter is that part of a space shuttle which carries astronauts and the cargo. It has cabins and beds inside it. Unmanned missions are remote-controlled spacecraft used to gather information about objects in space. Sputnik 1 was the first successful unmanned mission. It was sent into space on 4 October, 1957.

The rocket helps to lift the shuttle and push it into space.

Believe me!!!

The first living creature to travel into space was a dog called Laika. The spacecraft which carried her on 3 November, 1957 was called Sputnik 2.

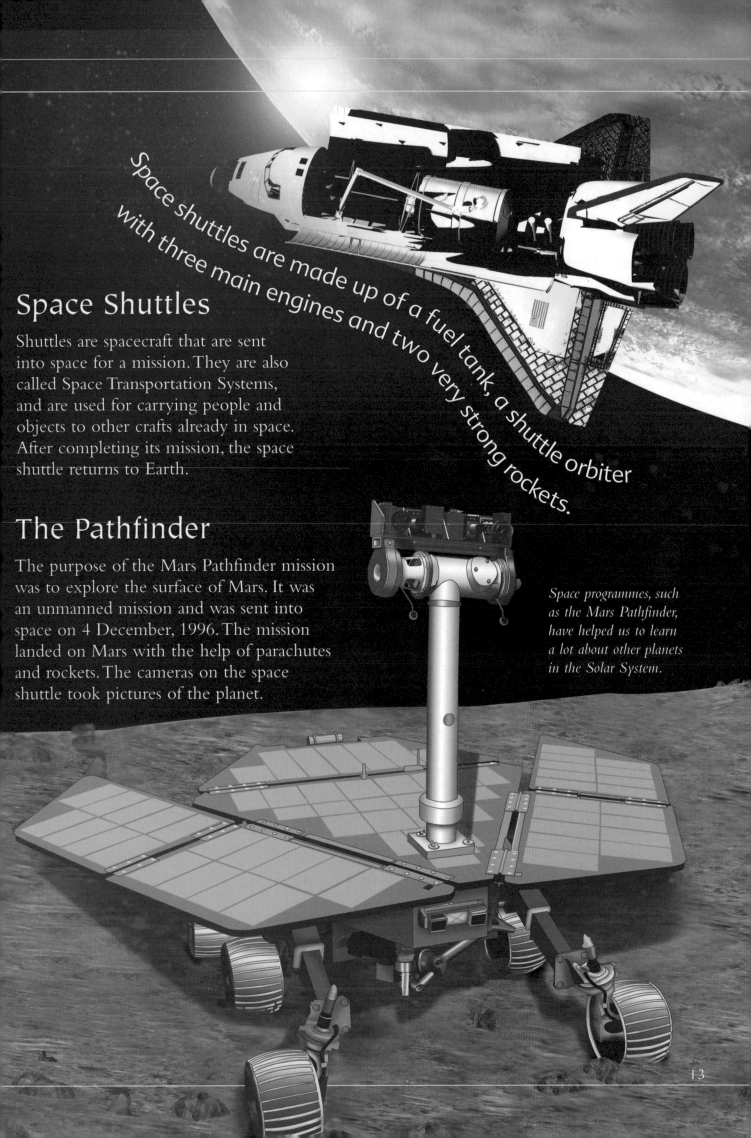

Space shuttles are made up of a fuel tank, a shuttle orbiter with three main engines and two very strong rockets.

Space Shuttles

Shuttles are spacecraft that are sent into space for a mission. They are also called Space Transportation Systems, and are used for carrying people and objects to other crafts already in space. After completing its mission, the space shuttle returns to Earth.

The Pathfinder

The purpose of the Mars Pathfinder mission was to explore the surface of Mars. It was an unmanned mission and was sent into space on 4 December, 1996. The mission landed on Mars with the help of parachutes and rockets. The cameras on the space shuttle took pictures of the planet.

Space programmes, such as the Mars Pathfinder, have helped us to learn a lot about other planets in the Solar System.

OUR PLANET

The Earth is the fifth largest planet and the third away from the s

Discover amazing facts about our planet. Take a trip back in time to see how continents were born, and learn about earthquakes, volcanoes, mountains and oceans.

Inside the Earth

When seen from space our planet looks like a giant blue marble. This is because most of the Earth's surface is covered with water. But deep inside, the Earth is full of hot, liquid rock.

Layers of the Earth

The Earth is made up of four main layers – the inner core, the outer core, the mantle and the crust. The inner core is at the centre of the Earth. It is made up of solid iron. The outer core comprises liquid iron and small amounts of nickel. The core is covered by the mantle, which is made up of melted rocks known as magma. The crust is the outermost layer. We live on the crust.

The Earth spins on its own axis as it revolves around the Sun.

The Earth is made up of many layers of rocks and minerals. The diagram below shows the different layers of the Earth. As one goes deeper into the Earth, the temperature rises.

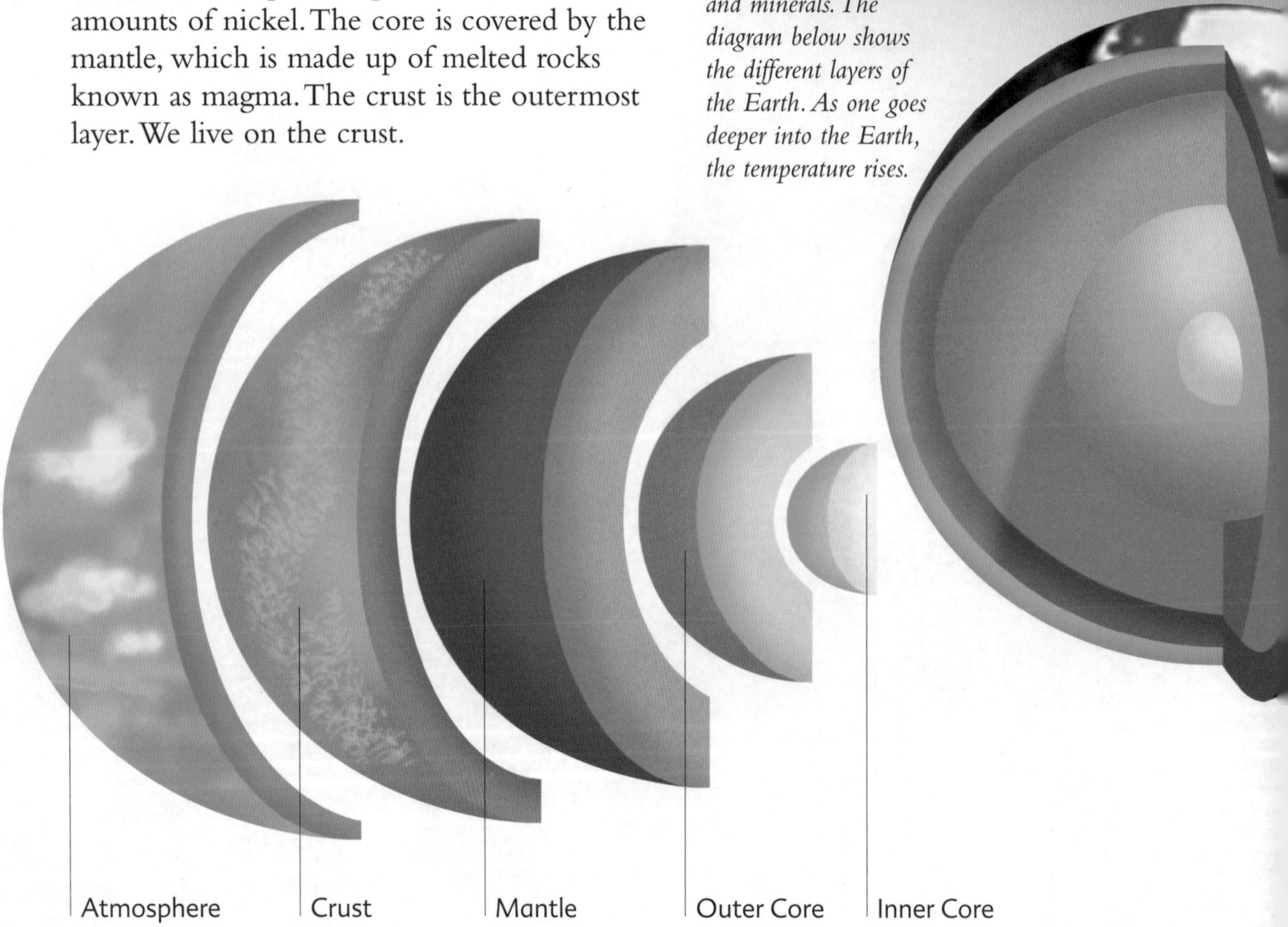

Atmosphere | Crust | Mantle | Outer Core | Inner Core

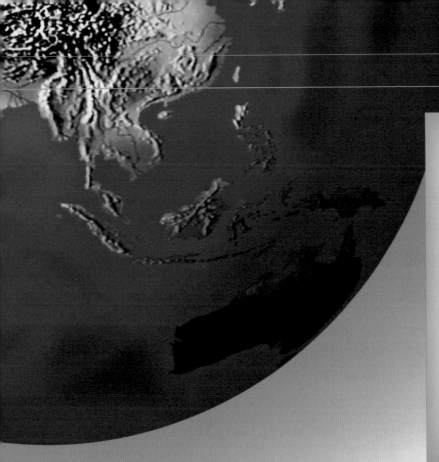

Word Wizard

Tectonic Plates: The Earth's crust is broken up into massive pieces of rock called tectonic plates. There are 12 large plates. The plates that form the ocean floor are called oceanic plates and the ones that form land are called continental plates.

Continents

Most of the land on the Earth's surface has been divided into seven huge masses called continents. These are North America, South America, Australia, Antarctica, Africa, Asia and Europe. Scientists believe that millions of years ago there was only one giant piece of land. They named this 'super-continent' Pangaea. It is said that the Pangaea broke up into smaller land masses. At first, it split into two huge pieces – Laurasia in the north and Gondwanaland in the south. Laurasia split further into North America, Europe and Asia, while Gondwanaland gave rise to South America, Africa, Australia and Antarctica.

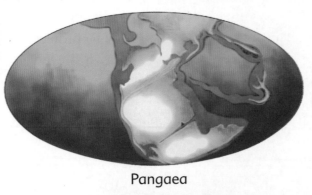

Pangaea

120 Million Years Ago

Over 250 Million Years ago

Present

17

Mount Kilauea in Hawaii, USA is said to be the most active volcano in the world.

Earthquakes and Volcanoes

Earthquakes, volcanoes, tsunamis and avalanches are types of natural disasters. Most natural disasters are caused by the movement of the Earth's crust, while others occur due to changes in weather.

Angry Earth

The plates, which make up the crust, sometimes separate or slide past each other in sudden rapid movements causing the Earth to shake. This is called an earthquake. Most earthquakes are so small that they can hardly be felt. But big earthquakes can make the ground shake very hard, leading to the collapse of houses and huge buildings.

Although the intensity of an earthquake can be measured, it is very difficult to predict an earthquake. However, we can be prepared for it. People who live in earthquake-prone cities learn how to protect themselves during emergencies. Today, it is even possible to construct buildings that can withstand earthquakes.

Mars has the largest volcano in the Solar System. It is called Olympus Mons and is 25.75 km high! This is almost three times the size of Mount Everest on Earth.

Believe me!!!

Volcanoes

Like earthquakes, volcanic eruptions too are caused by the movement of the Earth's tectonic plates. Most volcanoes are found on the edges of these plates. When one plate slides below the other, the heat in the Earth's mantle causes the lower plate to melt. The melted rocks and gases then force their way through cracks in the surface, causing volcanic eruptions.

Geysers and hot springs are formed when water seeps into the earth, then erupts through cracks in the Earth's crust.

The specially designed Transamerica Pyramid building survived the 1989 earthquake of San Francisco.

Tsunamis

Earthquakes and eruptions under the oceans cause tsunamis. These giant waves can travel thousands of kilometres over the seas at great speeds. Tsunamis are also known as tidal waves.

The Tusamis that hit Southeast Asia o_ 26 December, 2004 destroyed cities, seaside communities and holiday resorts. Tens of thousands of people in a dozen countries were killed. This was the world's most powerful earthquake in more than 40 years.

Avalanches

Avalanches are large masses of snow, ice and mud sliding down a mountain. They are usually caused by heavy snowfall. Earthquakes too can cause an avalanche. When the ground shakes, it frees a large amount of snow and rock causing it to slide down mountainsides. People who are out in the open during avalanches can get buried under tons of snow. Rescuing victims involves searching the area for clues, such as knapsacks, skiing equipment or pieces of clothing.

Rescue dogs have a very strong sense of smell. They can locate people buried under the snow as deep as four metres.

Natural Features

Mountains, valleys, plains, plateaus, rivers and lakes are some of the natural features of the Earth. These natural features play an important role in deciding the weather of a region, and the kinds of animals and plants that are found there.

Mountains

A mountain is formed when two large pieces of the Earth's rocky crust push hard against each other. Some mountains are formed by volcanic eruptions. In fact, some of the highest mountains in the world are volcanoes.

The weather on top of mountains is very cold and windy. Despite this, many people and animals live in the mountains.

Oceans

About 70 per cent of the Earth's surface is covered by water. The water in the oceans is very salty and cannot be used for drinking. But the ocean is home to several kinds of fish and other fascinating creatures. The Atlantic, Pacific, Indian, Arctic and Antarctic oceans are the five oceans of the world.

The surface under the oceans forms the ocean floor. This surface has been divided into several parts, such as continental shelf, continental slope, trenches and sea mounts. Continental shelf is the part of the sea shore that is underwater. The shelf slowly drops deeper into the ocean, forming the continental slope. Trenches are deep pits in the ocean floor. Oceans also contain mountains that are taller than even Mount Everest!

Continental Shelf | Continental Slope | Sea Mount | Mid-Ocean Ridges | Deep Sea Trench

Mount Everest, the world's highest mountain on land, is a part of the Himalayan range in South Asia. It is 8,848 metres high.

Word Wizard

Plateau: A large area of land that is separated from surrounding land by steep slopes. Most plateaus are on a higher level than their surroundings. But some, like the Tibetan Plateau, lie between mountains.

Valleys, Caves and Plains

The Earth's surface also consists of valleys and plains. A valley is a hollow surrounded by mountains or hills. Caves are large holes in the ground or in cliffs. There are several types of caves. Sea caves are formed when waves crash against cliffs and erode the rocks. But most caves are formed when rainwater or river water seeps into tiny cracks in huge rocks and erodes them. Plains are huge stretches of land that do not rise above the ground. They are usually lower than the land around them and mostly level.

Rivers and Lakes

Rivers are formed when rainwater or melted snow flows down as streams from a hill or a mountain. Several such streams flow into a channel to make a river. Rivers finally enter the ocean.

Lakes are formed when river water or rainwater is collected in large hollows in the ground. Most lakes contain fresh water. But some lakes, like Lake Eyre in Australia, contain salt water.

These natural sandstone rocks in Utah, USA eroded over thousands of years to take on the appearance of sculpted statues.

21

Climate and Weather

When winds start spinning at a very fast speed, a tornado is born.

Ever wonder why some days are hot while others are cold? This is due to changes in climate and weather. Both climate and weather affect our daily lives.

Climate

Climate is the kind of weather that a place has throughout the year. The climate of a particular place depends upon its distance from the Earth's equator. Places that lie close to the equator have hot, tropical climates. These regions have rain almost every day! Places where summers are not too hot and winters are not too cold are said to have temperate climates. The climate in desert regions is dry throughout the year. It is cold and windy in the mountains, while polar regions are extremely cold.

Weather

Weather varies from day to day. It is caused by the Sun, which heats up certain parts of the Earth more than others. This unequal heating causes differences in air pressure. Air moves from hotter regions to cooler places. This movement causes changes in weather.

Believe me!!!

In summer, the North and South Poles have daylight for three months, and no night-time. In winter, they have three months of darkness. This is caused by the angle of Earth towards the Sun.

Sometimes you can see an arc of colours in the sky. This is called a rainbow and can generally be seen after it has rained. Rainbows are caused when sunlight shines through a raindrop. The colours of the arc are red, orange, yellow, green, blue, indigo and violet.

Seasons

The Earth is tilted to one side. So, as the Earth goes around the Sun, different places get different amounts of heat. This gives rise to changes in seasons. The weather in a region also changes with the seasons. Most places have four seasons - spring, summer, autumn and winter.

Weather Forecast

Do you know what all the weather symbols mean?

This symbol indicates sunny weather. Without sunshine, there would be no weather.

When vapour freezes into tiny ice crystals, it combines with cooler water drops and falls as snow.

This one stands for cloudy weather. Clouds are formed when water vapour cools and turns into water droplets.

When the clouds become heavy, the water droplets fall back to the Earth as rain. This symbol above indicates stormy weather.

In autumn, there is not enough sunlight for leaves to feed themselves and stay green. They change to reds, browns and yellows before they finally shed.

23

THE NATURAL WORLD

Only seven per cent of the Earth
yet 80 per cent of the world's plan

Explore the deserts,
rainforests and
polar regions. Enter
a world filled with
wonderful animals,
birds and plants.

surface is covered by rainforests,
species are found here

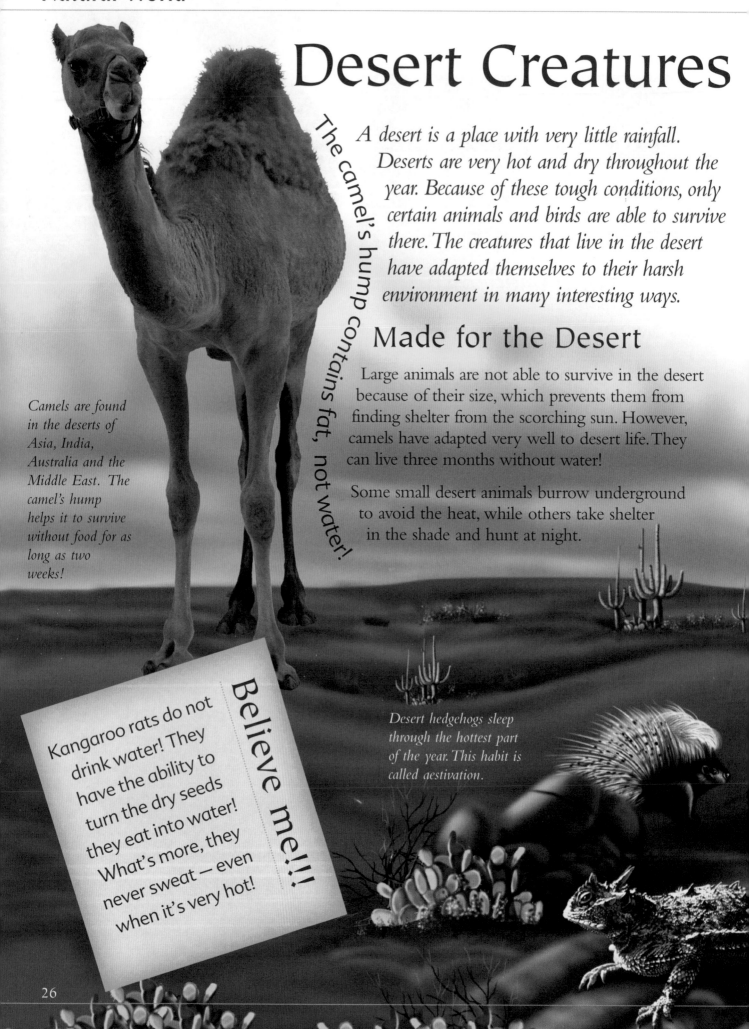

Desert Creatures

A desert is a place with very little rainfall. Deserts are very hot and dry throughout the year. Because of these tough conditions, only certain animals and birds are able to survive there. The creatures that live in the desert have adapted themselves to their harsh environment in many interesting ways.

The camel's hump contains fat, not water!

Made for the Desert

Large animals are not able to survive in the desert because of their size, which prevents them from finding shelter from the scorching sun. However, camels have adapted very well to desert life. They can live three months without water!

Some small desert animals burrow underground to avoid the heat, while others take shelter in the shade and hunt at night.

Camels are found in the deserts of Asia, India, Australia and the Middle East. The camel's hump helps it to survive without food for as long as two weeks!

Desert hedgehogs sleep through the hottest part of the year. This habit is called aestivation.

Kangaroo rats do not drink water! They have the ability to turn the dry seeds they eat into water! What's more, they never sweat — even when it's very hot!

Believe me!!!

26

Who Lives There?

The desert is home to a variety of creatures. Apart from camels, the most commonly found animals include kangaroos, prairie dogs, rattlesnakes, vipers, hedgehogs, scorpions and different kinds of insects. Lizards, such as the horned lizard and the western banded gecko, also live here.

The desert also has a number of birds. They include ostriches, owls, road runners, hawks and vultures.

Kangaroo rats have small plump bodies and big eyes. They move around by hopping on their hind feet.

The great horned owl of North America gets its name from the tufts of feather on its head, which look like horns.

Prairie dogs are actually short, fat squirrels. They are called dogs because they make a sound like a dog's bark.

Polar Creatures

The two polar regions are the coldest on Earth. The Arctic (surrounding the North Pole) and Antarctic (surrounding the South Pole) are home to some fascinating species that can survive such a harsh climate.

Polar Ways

Despite the extreme cold, a great number of animals and birds can be found in the polar regions. Animals like polar bears, seals and walruses are commonly found here. These animals thrive in their extreme environment as they have ways of keeping themselves warm.

Some have layers of fat, while others like the polar bears and the Artic fox have thick fur. Certain fish and insects have special chemicals in their blood that stop them from freezing. The birds have waterproof feathers. Some animals even migrate to warmer places when it gets too cold.

Walruses have an almost hairless body, long tusks and moustache-like hair on the upper lip.

Polar Birds

When one thinks about the polar regions, one of the first things that come to mind is the penguin. But penguins are not the only birds that live in such cold climates. Several birds like Arctic terns and puffins can also be found in the region.

Frozen Ocean

The ocean in the polar regions is frozen for the most part. However, it also supports a number of life forms. Apart from the squid, the octopus and a wide range of fish, you will also find different kinds of whales, including the blue whale and various smaller creatures.

The Emperor penguin is the biggest penguin.

Killer whales are also known as orcas. They are black and white in colour and are very fast swimmers. They eat all sorts of sea animals, including seals, fish, seabirds and turtles.

Word Wizard

Carnivores: These are animals that eat flesh. The word carnivore is made up of two Latin words: *Caro* meaning 'flesh' and *vorare* meaning 'to swallow'. Lions, tigers, polar bears and killer whales are all carnivores.

Arctic foxes eat young seals and the leftovers of those animals killed by the polar bear.

Grasslands

Grasslands are dry, dusty stretches of land with very few trees. The climate here is hot for most of the year with heavy rainfall in between. Grasslands are found mainly in Asia, Africa, North America and South America. They are also known as savannas, prairies, or steppes. Most of the well-known animals and birds live in the grasslands.

No two zebras have the same pattern of stripes. Some scientists believe that zebras are social animals. Their stripes are like identity badges that help zebras to recognise one another!

Believe me!!!

King of the Jungle

The grasslands are home to many big cats like lions, cheetahs and leopards. Of these, the lion is the most feared. These large golden cats live in big groups called prides. A single pride may contain more than 15 lions. Lions usually hunt in groups. They eat zebras, antelopes and wildebeest. The male lion is very easily identifiable by his glorious mane.

The cheetah is the fastest animal on land, reaching a top speed of about 112 km/h.

Elephants use their trunks to breathe and break leaves to eat.

Grassland Animals

The animals that live in the grasslands love the rainy season, which lasts for about eight months. During the dry season most animals migrate to neighbouring regions in search of water. Some burrowing animals sleep through the dry season. The typical grassland animals include elephants, zebras, rhinos, cheetahs, gazelles, leopards, lions, warthogs, giraffes and hippopotamus, to name a few.

Grassland Birds

The grasslands also have birds of various species. Three kinds of flightless birds live in the grasslands of the world. They are the ostrich, the rhea and the emu. Vultures, hawks and hornbills too can be found here. Other than these the grasslands are home to many smaller birds, such as larks, pipits, finches and fly-catchers.

Giraffes have extremely long necks that help them to reach leaves higher up on trees.

African elephants are the largest animals on land, even bigger than the Asian elephant. They have huge ears and large tusks.

31

The Rainforest

Rainforests are thick jungles near the Earth's equator. It is hot and humid here and rains for most of the year. More than half of all known kinds of plants and animals live in rainforests.

The American alligator

Rainforest Animals

Tropical rainforests provide constant warmth and a great deal of water and food for the animals that live here. The most common rainforest animals include small monkeys, snakes, lizards, alligators, rodents, insects and frogs.

Jaguars are large wild cats that are very strong. They live in caves, but can climb trees and swim very well. Tigers, the biggest wild cats on the planet, are also found in rainforests.

The boa constrictor is a large snake that kills its prey by squeezing it to death. It eats birds, lizards, small monkeys and rodents.

Word Wizard

Reptiles: These are animals that have dry, scaly skin and can lay eggs. There are many different kinds of reptiles in the world. Crocodiles, snakes, lizards and turtles are all reptiles.

grows up to 3.5 metres; the Chinese alligator grows up to 1.8 metres.

Rainforest Reptiles

One of the most interesting creatures of the rainforest is the anaconda, or water boa. It is the world's biggest snake and can grow to almost 11 metres! Another interesting rainforest reptile is the alligator. It looks like a crocodile and can live on both land and water.

Rainforest Birds

The birds of the rainforests are indeed very colourful. The toucan, a small bird with a colourful beak, is a common rainforest resident. Apart from the toucan you will also find macaws, parrots, hummingbirds, eagles, owls and quetzals in rainforests.

Macaws are brightly coloured, with a big beak and a long tail.

Ocean Life

Oceans are home to a large number of fascinating creatures. From the colourful coral fish to mean-looking sharks and the huge blue whale, animals of all shapes and sizes live in the ocean.

Fish

The ocean contains more than 20,000 different species of fish. However, fish can be broadly divided into two types – bony and cartilaginous fish. Most fish, except for sharks and rays, belong to the first group. Both sharks and rays have no bones in their body! Instead, their skeleton is made up of cartilage. The whale shark is the largest fish in the world!

Coral Reefs

Coral reefs look like gardens at the bottom of the ocean. They are colourful and are home to several ocean creatures like sea turtles, hermit crabs, lobsters, sea anemones and starfish. A wide range of colourful fish are also found near the reefs.

The largest animal on Earth is the blue whale. Its throat is so big that it starts from the mouth and ends at the stomach. What's more, the blue whale's heart is the size of a small car!

Believe me!!!

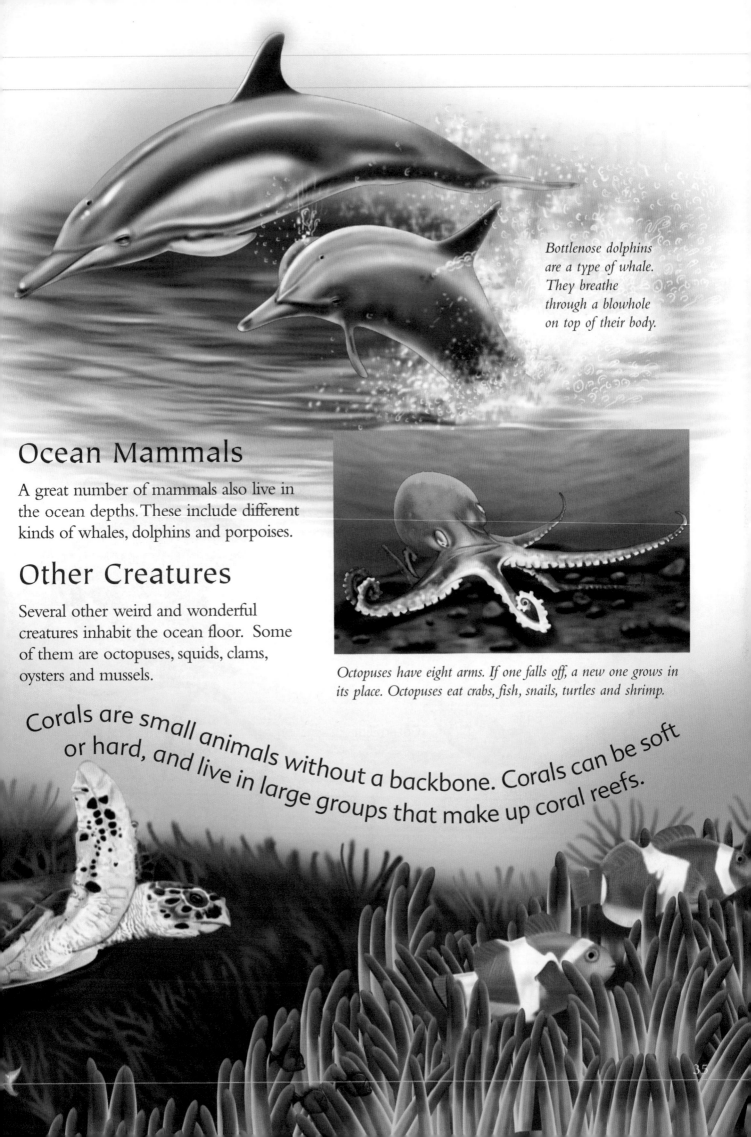

Bottlenose dolphins are a type of whale. They breathe through a blowhole on top of their body.

Ocean Mammals

A great number of mammals also live in the ocean depths. These include different kinds of whales, dolphins and porpoises.

Other Creatures

Several other weird and wonderful creatures inhabit the ocean floor. Some of them are octopuses, squids, clams, oysters and mussels.

Octopuses have eight arms. If one falls off, a new one grows in its place. Octopuses eat crabs, fish, snails, turtles and shrimp.

Corals are small animals without a backbone. Corals can be soft or hard, and live in large groups that make up coral reefs.

35

The World of Insects

The number of different species of insects is greater than all the other animals combined. Some insects like cockroaches, locusts and termites are harmful. They spread diseases, destroy crops and furniture. Insects like bees and butterflies are helpful. They spread pollen between plants and help them to reproduce.

Insect Body

Insects are invertebrates, meaning, they do not have backbones. But they have six legs and two antennae. Some insects have two pairs of wings too! The body of an insect is divided into three parts – head, thorax and abdomen.

Insect Lifecycle

All insects lay eggs. Some insects, such as grasshoppers and bugs, don't change much during their life. But other insects, such as butterflies, have complex lifecycles. The egg of a butterfly hatches into a caterpillar, which looks more like a worm and does not resemble the adult in any way. The caterpillar feeds on leaves and grows. It then spins a hard outer cover called a pupa around its body. The caterpillar changes into a butterfly or a moth inside this pupa.

Adult Butterfly

Eggs

Caterpillar

Pupa about to open

Pupa

Adult butterfly coming out of pupa

The lifecycle of a swallowtail butterfly illustrates the typical stages of growth in butterflies.

Some beetles are harmful, while others are not. Longhorn beetles bore holes into the trunks of trees in search of food, thus destroying the tree.

The praying mantis camouflages itself and waits for its prey to approach. It does not move until the prey comes close. Then, the mantis grabs the prey with its sharp, spiny front legs.

Attack and Defence

Most insects are brightly coloured. Butterflies and moths have different patterns on their bodies that scare their enemies away. Some insects, like the leaf and stick insects, use camouflage to protect themselves. But certain insects like the praying mantis uses camouflage to capture prey. Shield bugs, or stink bugs, produce a foul-smelling liquid when attacked!

Social Insects

Certain insects live in huge colonies. These include ants, termites, bees and wasps. The members of the colonies are divided according to their tasks. For example the queen lays the eggs, while the workers hunt for food. Soldier ants or bees defend the colony.

Word Wizard

Camouflage: The ability of some creatures to blend into their surroundings. For example, some insects like the stick insect live on trees. They are brown in colour and look like dried twigs.

Ants work in teams to lift heavy things. Ants can carry 10-20 times their body weight.

The Greenhouse

Plants grow in our gardens, in deserts, forests, even in oceans and seas! There are over 300,000 different kinds of plants. They include trees, shrubs, vines, flowers and bushes.

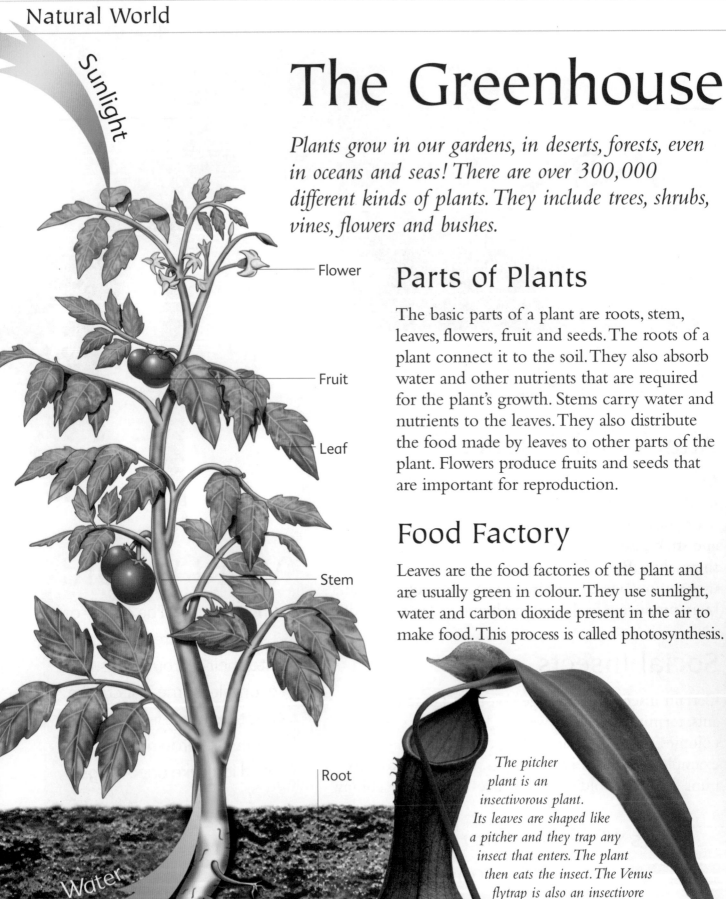

Sunlight

Flower

Fruit

Leaf

Stem

Root

Water

Parts of Plants

The basic parts of a plant are roots, stem, leaves, flowers, fruit and seeds. The roots of a plant connect it to the soil. They also absorb water and other nutrients that are required for the plant's growth. Stems carry water and nutrients to the leaves. They also distribute the food made by leaves to other parts of the plant. Flowers produce fruits and seeds that are important for reproduction.

Food Factory

Leaves are the food factories of the plant and are usually green in colour. They use sunlight, water and carbon dioxide present in the air to make food. This process is called photosynthesis.

The pitcher plant is an insectivorous plant. Its leaves are shaped like a pitcher and they trap any insect that enters. The plant then eats the insect. The Venus flytrap is also an insectivore and, like the pitcher plant, eats insects. The Bladderwort, a carnivorous plant, is found in the water. The leaves of this plant catch small animals for it to eat.

The fruits of many plants form an important part of our diet. Some common fruits are apples, pears, bananas and oranges.

Flower to Flower

Flowers are responsible for the birth of new plants. Most flowers have two parts. The male part, called stamen, surrounds the female part, or pistil. Flowers are pretty for a reason. Their bright colours attract birds and insects, which carry the pollen from one flower to another. When the pollen falls on the pistil, seeds are formed. Later, these seeds grow into new plants.

Onions grow in the ground. Both their leaves and bulbs can be eaten.

The green shoots and stems of the asparagus plant can be eaten.

The flowers of plants like broccoli and cauliflower are popular for their nutritive qualities.

Lettuce leaves are commonly eaten as part of salads.

39

Oaks are big trees found in deciduous forests. Their wood is very hard and is used for construction.

Plants are found in almost all parts of the world and in all kinds of climate – blazing hot or freezing cold! Just like animals, plants too adapt themselves to their extreme living conditions.

Water lilies are found in water and have beautiful flowers in many colours like blue, yellow, white and pink.

Aquatic Plants

Plants that are submerged in, or float on, water also have special features that help them to adapt to their surroundings. Plants under water do not have the protective layer required to prevent water loss. These plants have small or no roots but they have air cavities in their leaves and stems that provide the necessary air. Floating plants have thick, waxy leaves with pores on the upper surface. The waxy substance resists water, thus keeping the pores open all the time.

Word Wizard

Succulent plants: These are plants that have very juicy and fleshy tissue or stems. The stem can absorb a lot of water, which is stored for future use. Succulent plants, such as the cactus, are usually found in the desert.

Arctic Plants

Plants are rare in the polar regions, especially in the continent of Antarctica. Only plants such as lichens and mosses are found here. But, the Arctic tundra supports the growth of flowering plants. Trees, however, cannot grow in such extreme conditions. Only plants that grow close to the ground can survive in the tundra. Arctic plants have smaller leaves that help to retain moisture. Some plants even have fur to keep them warm! Most Arctic plants, especially flowering plants, bloom during spring and summer.

The flowers of the Arctic poppy keep turning through the day to catch the Sun's rays.

Desert Plants

Plants require water to survive. But water is very hard to come by in the desert. So desert plants, like the cactus, have no leaves. Instead, they have thick juicy stems that prevent the loss of water. Some have extremely long roots that go deep into the ground in search of water. Some desert plants 'sleep' through the dry summer, while others spring up for a short period after heavy rainfall.

Tropical Rainforests

Tropical rainforests have very thick vegetation. The tall trees in these regions prevent sunlight from reaching the ground. The survival of a plant in the rainforests depends upon how the plant adapts itself to constant shade. Plants like the strangler fig grow on other plants and trees in order to reach the sunlight. Some of these plants that grow high above the ground have long roots that draw water from the ground. Others have roots growing out of their stems. These aerial roots absorb moisture from the air.

The thick woody stems of the cactus perform the function of leaves. The stems contain chlorophyll, which makes the process of photosynthesis possible.

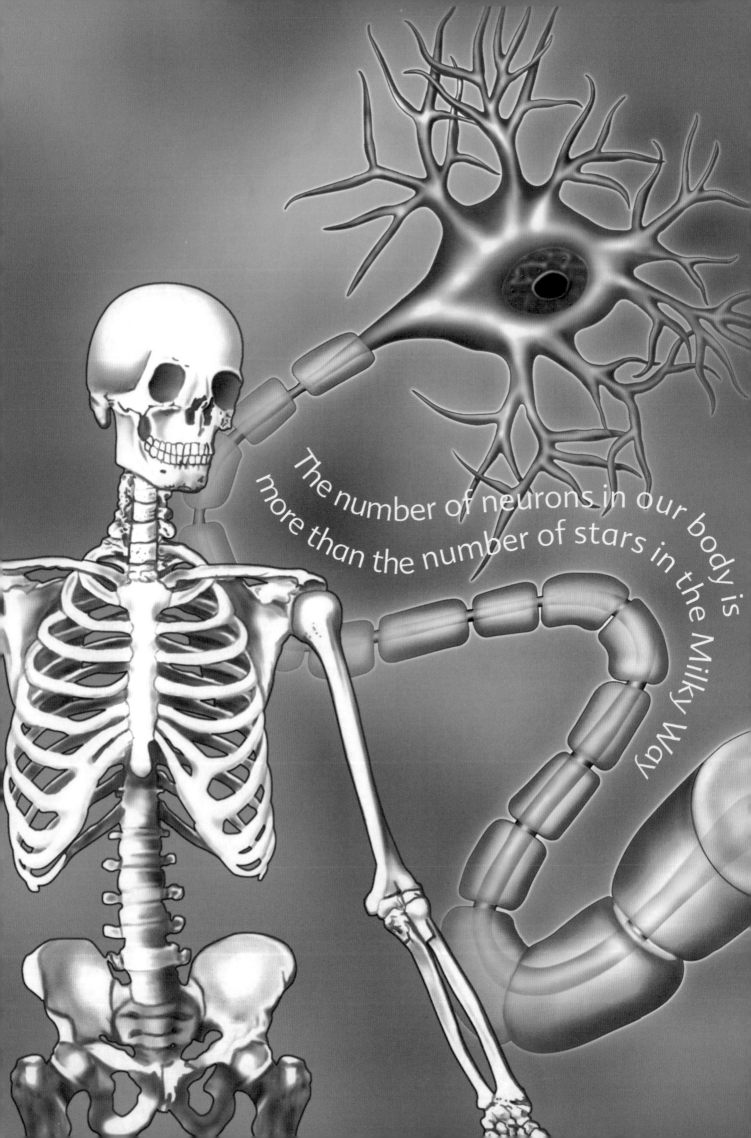

The number of neurons in our body is more than the number of stars in the Milky Way

THE HUMAN BODY

Take a look inside our body and find out how we breathe, what happens to the food we eat and how the different parts of our body work.

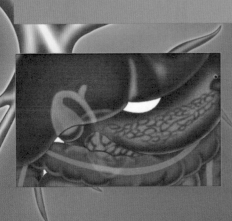

Parts of the Body

The human body is an amazing machine. It is made up of various organs, bones and muscles. All of these work together to help us move, talk, see, eat and breathe!

Bones

There are 206 bones in our body. These bones form the skeleton, which gives our body shape and structure. Bones contain calcium and phosphorous and are hard. The points at which two bones meet are called joints. These help us to move various parts of our body. Teeth are also a part of the skeleton. They give our face shape and are covered by enamel. The teeth are the hardest part of the human body.

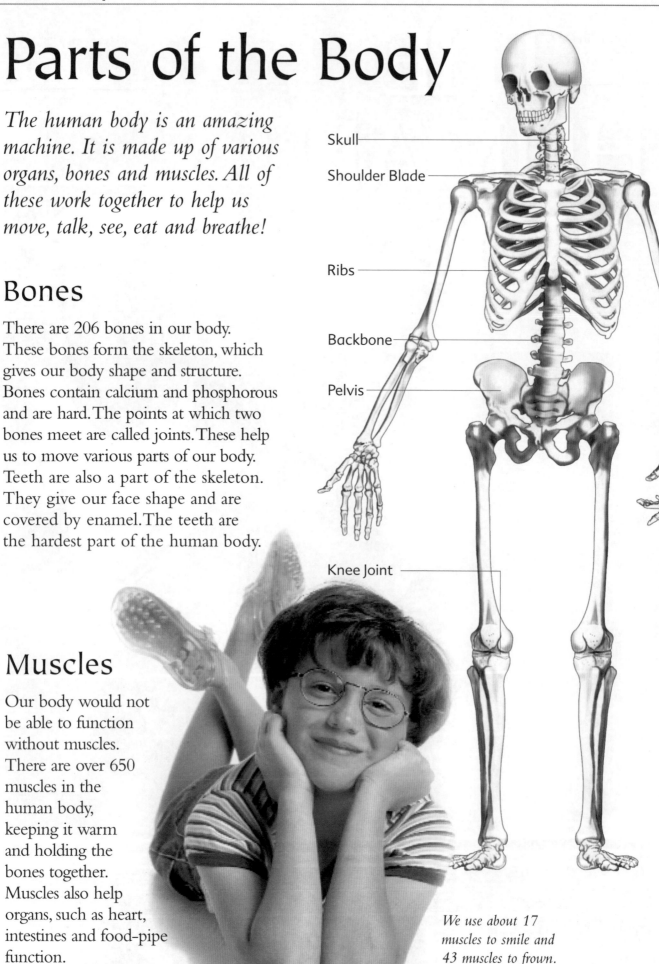

Skull

Shoulder Blade

Ribs

Backbone

Pelvis

Knee Joint

Muscles

Our body would not be able to function without muscles. There are over 650 muscles in the human body, keeping it warm and holding the bones together. Muscles also help organs, such as heart, intestines and food-pipe function.

We use about 17 muscles to smile and 43 muscles to frown.

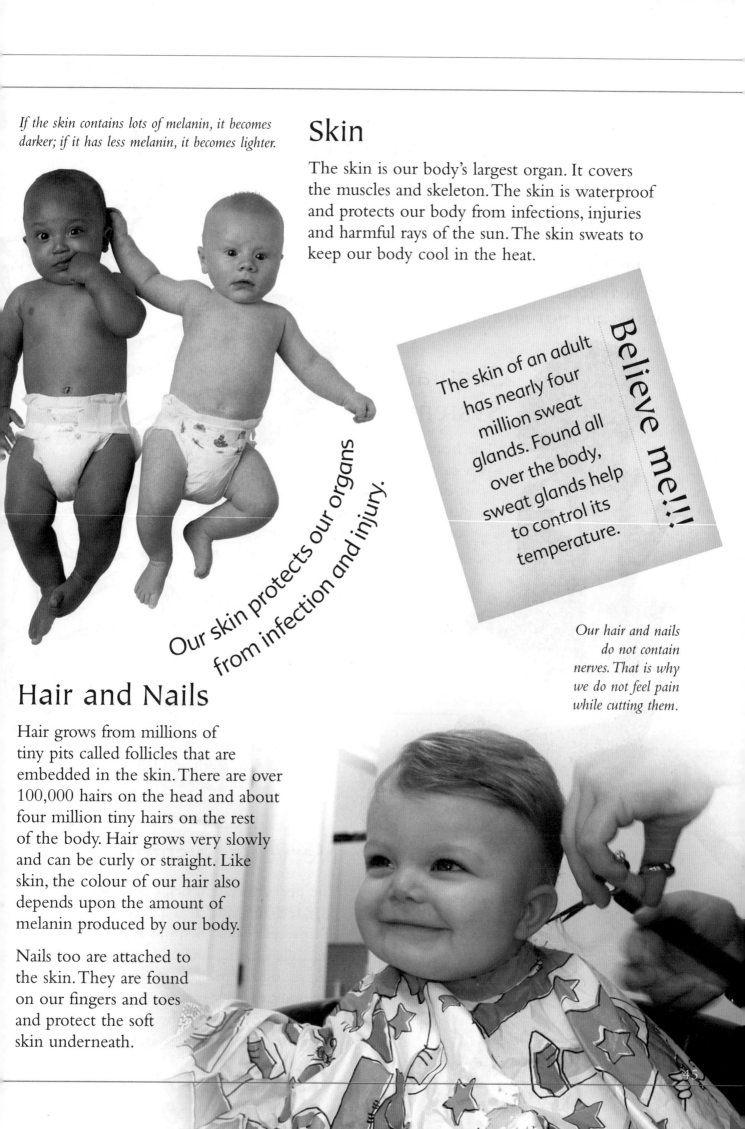

If the skin contains lots of melanin, it becomes darker; if it has less melanin, it becomes lighter.

Skin

The skin is our body's largest organ. It covers the muscles and skeleton. The skin is waterproof and protects our body from infections, injuries and harmful rays of the sun. The skin sweats to keep our body cool in the heat.

Our skin protects our organs from infection and injury.

The skin of an adult has nearly four million sweat glands. Found all over the body, sweat glands help to control its temperature.

Believe me!!!

Our hair and nails do not contain nerves. That is why we do not feel pain while cutting them.

Hair and Nails

Hair grows from millions of tiny pits called follicles that are embedded in the skin. There are over 100,000 hairs on the head and about four million tiny hairs on the rest of the body. Hair grows very slowly and can be curly or straight. Like skin, the colour of our hair also depends upon the amount of melanin produced by our body.

Nails too are attached to the skin. They are found on our fingers and toes and protect the soft skin underneath.

Body Mechanics

There are various systems inside our body that help it to function efficiently. A system is a group of organs that carry out similar tasks. Our body consists of circulatory, respiratory, digestive and nervous systems.

Nucleus

Circulatory System

The heart and the channel that carries the blood are a part of this system. The heart pumps blood, which reaches other parts of the body, through a network of tubes called blood vessels. Blood vessels include arteries, veins and capillaries. Arteries carry blood from the heart to other parts of the body, while veins carry the blood back to the heart. Capillaries are tiny blood vessels that can reach small areas, such as nails, eyes, ears, teeth and hair roots.

Nervous System

The nervous system helps us to see, hear, feel and taste. It is a network of tiny cells called neurons and is controlled by the brain. Neurons carry electric signals from various parts of our body, such as eyes, ears, nose and tongue, to our brain. The brain then helps us to identify these signals.

Our eyes stay the same size throughout our life. But our ears and nose do not stop growing!

Respiratory System

This system consists of the nose, wind pipe and the lungs. When we breathe, air travels through the nose and wind pipe to enter the lungs. The blood in the lungs absorbs the oxygen and carries it to other parts of the body. Similarly, when we breathe out, carbon dioxide is expelled from our body.

Digestive system

Our body gets its energy from the food we eat. But the food has to be broken down into smaller pieces before our body can absorb the nutrients in it. This process of breaking down food is called digestion. The digestive system consists of the mouth, food pipe, stomach, intestine and anus. The food is broken down in stages as it passes through this digestive tract. The unwanted substances are pushed out of our body as urine or solid waste.

Around 1.7 litres of saliva is produced in the mouth every day!

— Mouth

— Food Pipe

— Liver

— Stomach

— Small Intestine

— Large Intestine

— Anus

Word Wizard

Urine: It is the liquid waste that leaves the body through the kidneys. Urine consists of water, salts and wastes that are harmful to our body. Urine is often yellowish in colour.

SCIENCE &
TECHNOLOGY

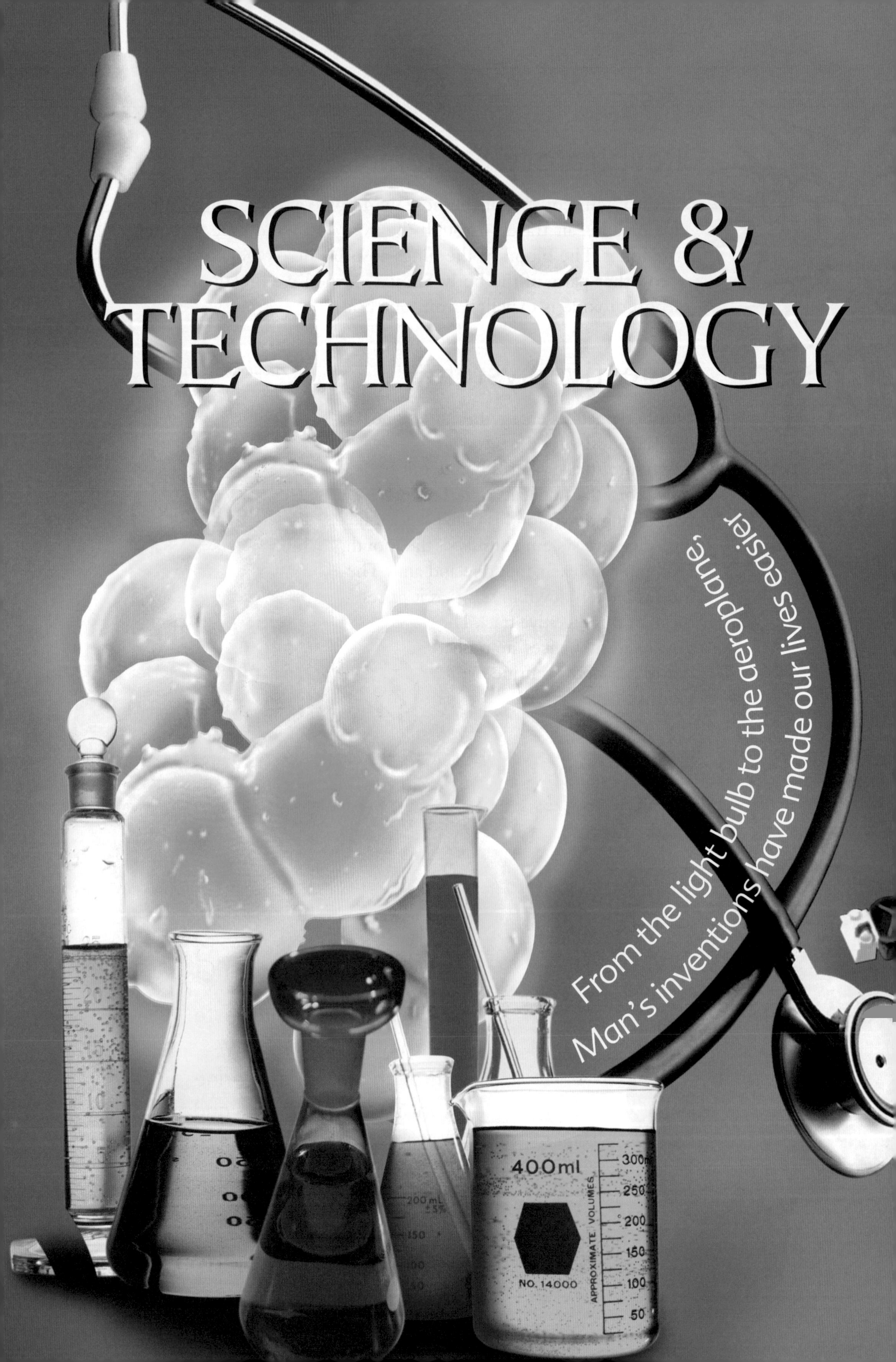

From the light bulb to the aeroplane, Man's inventions have made our lives easier

400ml

300ml

250

200

APPROXIMATE VOLUMES

150

100

50

NO. 14000

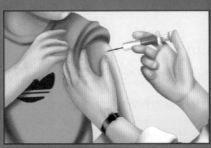

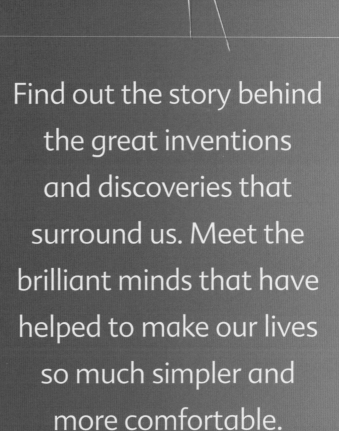
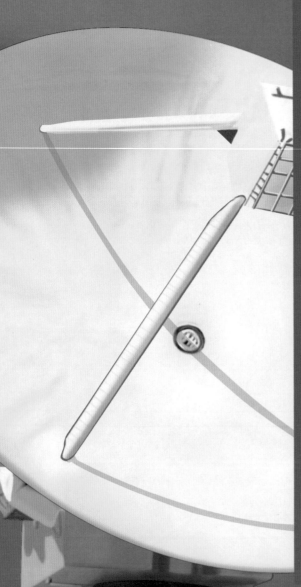

Find out the story behind the great inventions and discoveries that surround us. Meet the brilliant minds that have helped to make our lives so much simpler and more comfortable.

Energy and Power

Energy is all around us in many different forms. There are several sources of energy, such as the sun, wind, water and fuel. Energy from the sun, wind and water can be reused, so it is called renewable energy. Non-renewable energy is obtained from nuclear power and fuels like oil and coal.

Solar Energy

Energy from the Sun is called solar energy. This energy can be converted into both heat and electricity. Today, solar energy is used for several things, such as heating water, generating electricity and even cooking food!

Wind

Wind is another common form of energy. Windmills work with the help of power that is created by wind. Windmills have been used for thousands of years to pump water and grind grain in mills. They are now even used to generate electricity!

Electricity is one of the most important forms of energy. Can you imagine a world without lights, refrigerators, television and computers? Electricity powers all of those things, as well as washing machines, radios, light bulbs, ovens, etc.

Water

Water is the oldest and most common source of renewable energy. The energy of flowing water is used to rotate giant turbines, which in turn activate huge generators in order to produce electricity.

Non-renewable Energy

This form of energy is produced by fuels like oil, petrol, natural gas and coal. Energy derived from burning wood also falls under this category. This energy is used to generate heat and electricity and move vehicles.

How does electricity reach us? It begins its journey at a power plant or generating station. Oil, gas or coal is burnt here to create heat. This heat is then changed into electricity, which travels along wires to our homes.

Coal-fired power plants generate electricity, but they are not very good for the environment. They produce toxic chemicals and gases, which are unhealthy for life on Earth.

Electricity travels through wires that either run below the ground or hang high in the air from metal towers called pylons.

The Hoover Dam in the USA is one of the world's biggest dams. It is 221 metres tall and 379 metres long. The dam aids the production of electricity for the states of Nevada, Arizona and California.

Believe me!!!

51

Communication and Sound

We hear all kinds of sounds every day – from the soft rustling of leaves and chirping of birds to the different notes of music. Did you know that sound travels as a wave of energy? It travels at a speed of 1,199 kilometres per hour – which is very fast indeed!

Communication Satellite

Mobile phones have changed the way we communicate today. They allow us to talk to people, play games and listen to music. We can even watch video clips on our mobile phones.

Communication

The most important use of sound is in communication, which plays a vital role in our daily lives. Both animals and humans use sound to communicate. However, sound is not the only form of communication. Writing a letter, watching television and sending e-mails are some common ways to share ideas, thoughts and information across the world.

Modes of Communication

The telephone is the most widely used instrument of communication in the world. It was invented by Alexander Graham Bell in 1876. But perhaps the most popular way to communicate today is through the computer. Computers can be used to write and send letters, talk to and see people in other parts of the world! Due to the Internet, the computer is now one of the most advanced sources of information and means of communication.

Radio and television also connect us to the rest of the world. We are able to view or listen to news and events almost as they happen. Isn't it amazing that one can learn about different countries and cultures at a push of a button?

Communication Technology

Have you ever wondered how you can watch an event that is taking place in another corner of the world from the comfort of your own living room? This is made possible by communication satellites. These are devices that are sent into space to transfer information from one part of the world to another. With the help of satellites, television and radio programmes can be shown and heard all over the planet. They also help us predict the weather. It is difficult to imagine a world without communication satellites!

Huge dish antennae send sounds and pictures to communication satellites, and receive the messages that are sent back.

Laptop computers are compact and can be carried around. The first recognised laptop was invented in 1981 by Adam Osborne.

Medicine

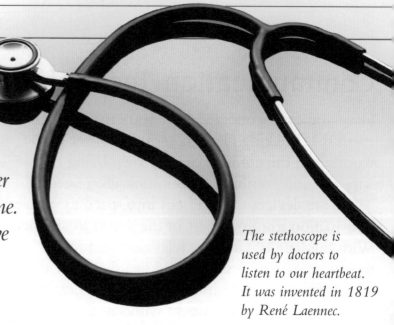

Some of the most important and valuable inventions and discoveries ever made have been in the field of medicine. Medical inventions have helped to save millions of lives by curing deadly diseases and preventing illness.

The stethoscope is used by doctors to listen to our heartbeat. It was invented in 1819 by René Laennec.

Microbes

Microbes are tiny disease-causing germs that cannot be seen by the naked eye. Bacteria and viruses are the most common microbes. They are the cause for most diseases – from common colds to life-threatening ones, such as cancer and AIDS.

Doctors to the Rescue

When you catch a cold or get hurt, you may go to a doctor. Have you noticed that the doctor uses different ways, such as listening to your heart or looking inside your mouth, to find out what exactly is wrong with you? This process is called diagnosis. In order to treat any disease, it is important to know the cause and nature of the disease. Some illnesses are easy to diagnose, like the common cold, however the diagnosis of serious and complicated diseases needs careful and deep study.

X-rays were invented by Wilhelm Conrad Roentgen in 1895. With X-rays, doctors can see our skeleton and find out if anything is wrong inside our body.

Treatment and Cure

After finding out the problem, the doctor recommends the most suitable medicines for cure. These could include pills or syrups. Sometimes the doctor might even inject the medicine into your body with a syringe.

Some diseases require surgery, or an operation. When this happens the patient is put to sleep so that the doctor can take a look inside the body and fix any problems he or she may find.

Vaccines protect us from dangerous diseases. All of us get vaccine injections or shots when we are children. Once we are vaccinated against a particular disease, we usually never catch that disease.

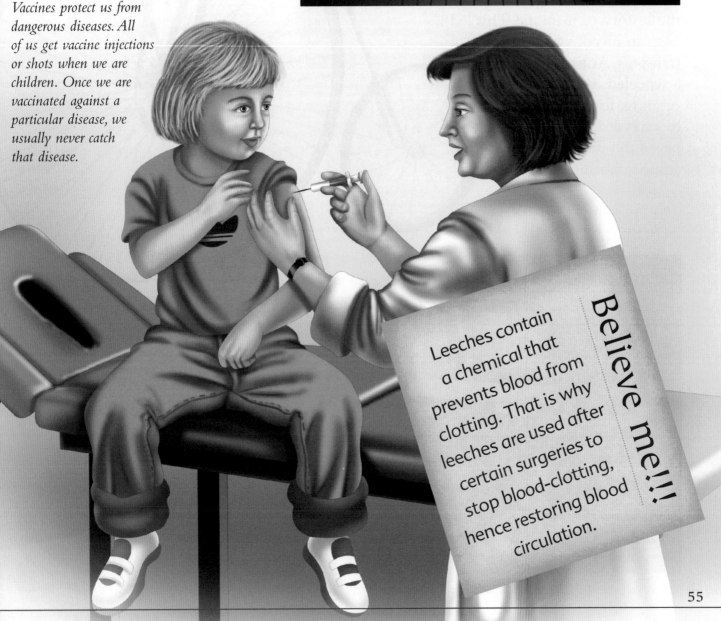

Leeches contain a chemical that prevents blood from clotting. That is why leeches are used after certain surgeries to stop blood-clotting, hence restoring blood circulation.

Believe me!!!

Transport

Throughout history, Man has been looking for faster and more comfortable ways to get from one place to another. This search has led us to invent different types of vehicles. There is now a wide choice of transportation that helps us travel across the seas, over land, and even through the air!

Early Transport

The invention of the wheel has been one of the most important events in the history of mankind. This led Man to invent various modes of transport. At first, he attached a wheeled cart to a horse or an ox for farming and to carry loads. This soon paved the way for more advanced vehicles.

In 1871, James Starley invented a bicycle called the Penny Farthing. This had one very large wheel in the front, a smaller wheel at the back, pedals and rubber tyres.

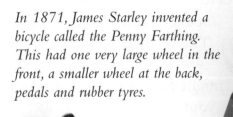

This three-wheeled vehicle is a popular mode of transport in India.

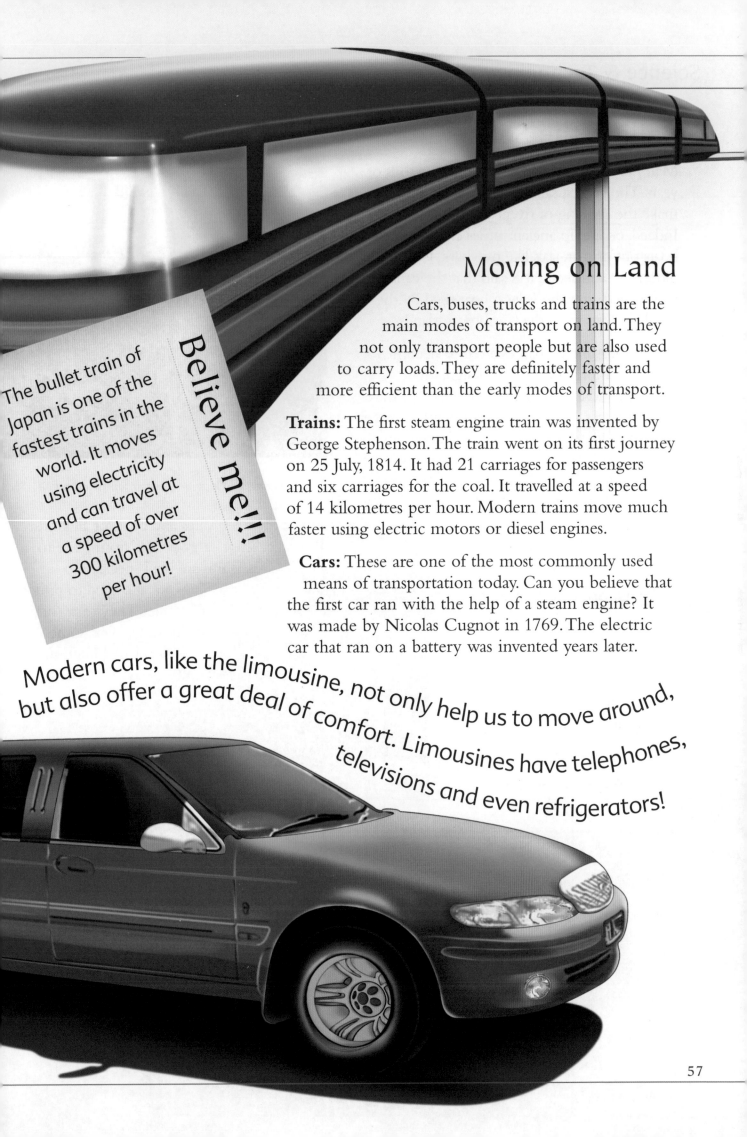

Moving on Land

Cars, buses, trucks and trains are the main modes of transport on land. They not only transport people but are also used to carry loads. They are definitely faster and more efficient than the early modes of transport.

Trains: The first steam engine train was invented by George Stephenson. The train went on its first journey on 25 July, 1814. It had 21 carriages for passengers and six carriages for the coal. It travelled at a speed of 14 kilometres per hour. Modern trains move much faster using electric motors or diesel engines.

Cars: These are one of the most commonly used means of transportation today. Can you believe that the first car ran with the help of a steam engine? It was made by Nicolas Cugnot in 1769. The electric car that ran on a battery was invented years later.

Believe me!!!

The bullet train of Japan is one of the fastest trains in the world. It moves using electricity and can travel at a speed of over 300 kilometres per hour!

Modern cars, like the limousine, not only help us to move around, but also offer a great deal of comfort. Limousines have telephones, televisions and even refrigerators!

Sailing the Seas

Man has been sailing the seas for thousands of years. The earliest sailing vessels were built to make the crossing of rivers and fishing easier. Indeed, people in ancient times cleverly crafted boats out of materials like tree bark, logs, animal hide, mud and reeds. It is said that the canoe was named after the *kanu*, a boat used by the Carib Indians from the Caribbean Islands.

With time, simple boats evolved to become faster and more complex in design. New materials and techniques and the need to travel long distances led to the development of bigger and better vessels. Steam power and engines replaced oars and sails to move vessels on water.

The gondolas of Venice are a major tourist attraction.

Today, there are ships and boats of all kinds. Passenger ships carry people from place to place. Cargo ships are built specially to transport goods. Ships are also used to protect a country from its enemies. They carry huge guns and missiles on board. In fact, some ships even carry fighter planes! Such ships are called aircraft carriers.

Word Wizard

Periscope: The periscope is a long vertical tube that has mirrors attached to both ends. It is used to see one's surroundings while remaining under the water. Submarines have periscopes.

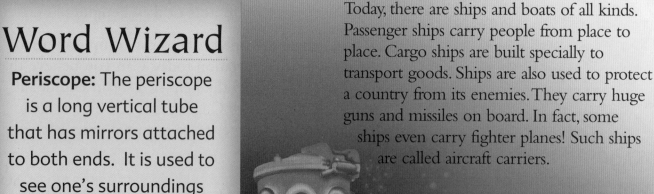

Submersibles are small vessels that are used by scientists for underwater exploration. These vessels help scientists study the ocean floor, underwater volcanoes and ocean life. They are also used to gather information about shipwrecks and aeroplane crashes.

Fly like a Bird...

Man has always longed to fly like a bird. Myths and legends from ancient times talk about various modes of flying. But this became a reality with the invention of the hot air balloon. These huge balloons are filled with hydrogen gas and have a basket attached to them by ropes.

The hot air balloon was invented by brothers Joseph and Jacques Montgolfier who demonstrated the first balloon flight on 5 June, 1783 in France. There were no people on board. The passengers of this flight were three animals – a sheep, a duck and a rooster.

Soon the craving to fly led to the invention of the aeroplane. The first aeroplane was invented by two brothers – Wilbur and Orville Wright. They took their first successful flight on 17 December, 1903. This flight lasted only 12 seconds. They flew at a height of three metres and covered a distance of 37 metres. Planes now fly thousands of kilometres in just a few hours.

Aeroplanes have made travelling easier and faster. Today, people can go from one place to another, in a different part of the world, in just a few hours.

The first balloon flight carrying people was made on 21 November, 1783.

FROM PAST TO PRESENT

From ancient cave-dwellings to the concrete jungles of the modern world, mankind has come a long way

Follow Man's journey from the earliest days to the discovery of the New World. Read about wars and revolutions, and visit kings, castles and different cultures.

Ancient Times

Until about 10,000 years ago, people simply wandered from one place to another in search of food and shelter. Gradually they learned to grow crops and rear animals. Soon, villages and towns were set up. People started to live in an organised society that had rulers, laws and different kinds of work.

Mesopotamians built huge 'stepped' structures like these called ziggurats. A temple of the city god was located on top of these ziggurats.

Seals from the Indus Valley civilisation show the script used during this period. Although the writings were short and simple, scientists have still not been able to understand or decode this script.

Mesopotamia

The Mesopotamian civilisation flourished on the banks of the Tigris and Euphrates rivers in Southwest Asia. The Mesopotamians built walls around their cities to protect themselves from enemies. They also built temples made of mud bricks. These were decorated with drawings and metalwork. Mesopotamia was ruled by various kings from the Sumerian, Babylonian and Assyrian dynasties.

Ancient India

The Indus Valley civilisation was the largest known in ancient times. It existed along the Indus River, which flows through India and Pakistan. Two of its most important cities were Mohenjo-Daro and Harappa. They had large forts or citadels on top of hills with huge houses and baths. The Great Bath of Mohenjo-Daro was around 13 metres long and seven metres wide. Bathing was not only a religious ritual but also a social event for the Indus Valley people. Around the citadels were small towns with streets, two-storeyed houses, markets and an advanced sewer system. The people here were also fond of art and pottery.

Shi Huangdi was the first emperor of United China.

Ancient China

The ancient Chinese civilisation was located on the banks of three major rivers – Chang Jiang, Xi Jiang and Huang He. Ancient China was ruled by several dynasties. Until 221 BC Ancient China was divided and war raged between the various chieftains. But the country was brought under one rule by Shi Huangdi of the Qin dynasty. Huangdi reorganised the government and introduced common systems of weights and money. He also started to build the Great Wall of China to protect his kingdom from invaders like the Huns. The Chinese started to make objects of iron during the rule of the Chou dynasty. Writing and literature also developed during this time.

Ancient Egypt

The Egyptian civilisation was based near the River Nile in the northeast of Africa. Egyptians were basically farmers. But they also studied mathematics and geometry, and practised medicine. Ancient Egyptians were great architects too. They built huge structures like the Pyramids, which are amongst the Seven Wonders of the World.

The Great Pyramid of Giza was built by the Egyptian pharaoh, Khufu around 2560 BC.

Word Wizard

Civilisation: A society that follows a common set of laws, and has developed political and religious organisations. Civilisations began when Man started to cultivate land and settle down in one place.

In one of the most famous battles fought on the banks of River Hydaspes, Alexander defeated Porus, a brave Indian king.

The Parthenon in Athens was designed by the two Greek architects, Ictinus and Callicrates.

Ancient Greece

Ancient Greek civilisation grew around the Mediterranean Sea. The Greeks were farmers and traders who usually travelled by sea. The Olympic Games, the world's greatest sporting event, were first held here. The people of Greece were interested in poetry, drama, sculpture and architecture. The Parthenon in Athens, dedicated to the Greek goddess Athena, is one of the most beautiful temples in the world. Some of the greatest scientists and thinkers like Socrates, Plato, Aristotle and Hippocrates were Greek. Alexander the Great was the most famous Greek ruler. He conquered Europe and parts of Asia, including India. The Greek culture spread far and wide under his rule.

The Egyptian city of Alexandria was named after Alexander the Great.

Ancient Rome

Ancient Rome was one of the most powerful empires in Europe. The Romans had big armies and conquered a large part of the neighbouring lands. They also built many towns with good roads, drains and temples. A huge stadium called the Coliseum, where gladiators used to fight, still stands today. It had marble seats and could hold 50,000 people!

The rich in Ancient Rome enjoyed many comforts. They wore expensive clothes and jewellery. They also held huge parties where they served many different kinds of food and wine. Most parties had entertainment, such as dancing and plays.

Ancient Americas

The people of the Mayan civilisation lived in Central America, which includes the present Mexico, Guatemala, El Salvador and Honduras among other nations. They were farmers and used to grow corn, avocados, pineapples, chilli peppers and cacao. They also built several temples and pyramids.

Religious beliefs of the Ancient Mayans were based on the stars; they built most of their temples according to the position of stars.

The Middle Ages

After the fall of the Roman Empire, the western and the eastern parts of the world went through a period of change. This period, known as the Middle Ages, saw many invasions as well as growth in art, music and culture.

Medieval Europe

Life in the Middle Ages was not easy. The people were divided according to their position in society. The king headed this social division called the feudal system. After him came the noblemen, such as barons, dukes and other important people. The king gave large parts of land to noblemen in exchange for the use of their soldiers in his army. The peasants, also known as serfs, lived on the nobleman's land and worked for him. The peasants had to pay high taxes and were almost like slaves to the lords.

Towns in the Middle Ages were usually located on crossings of roads or near rivers.

Word Wizard

Page and Squire: Pages were young boys training to become knights. When the page was 14 years old, he became a squire — servant of a knight. He learnt how to fight with a sword while riding a horse.

The word 'castle' comes from the Latin word 'castellum', meaning fortification, or something that strengthens.

Symbols of the English monarchy: the crown, the crest and the sceptre.

Castles of the Middle Ages

Apart from wars, the Middle Ages are also known for the castles built during this time. They were made mostly of stone and were usually surrounded by a canal of water. A drawbridge allowed people to enter and leave the castle. The walls of these castles were very thick and had small slits and holes in them through which the soldiers could shoot arrows or pour boiling oil onto the enemy below. Ouch!

A picture of a knight springs to mind at the mention of the Middle Ages. Knights were armed warriors who belonged to the nobility. They carried weapons, like lances and swords, rode horses and wore armour. The son of a lord was first made a page, then a squire and eventually he became a knight.

The Church

Another powerful part of medieval society was the Catholic Church. Religious leaders like the bishops were very powerful. Even kings and queens could not act without the permission of the Church. Several cathedrals were made during this period. Many important functions like the crowning of the king, christenings, weddings and burials were held in cathedrals.

The Samurai warriors of Japan were not only good swordsmen, they were also well-versed in the arts.

Medieval Asia

The Middle Ages did not affect Europe alone. Many countries in Asia also underwent historic changes. In India, the Middle Ages were marked by the arrival of the Mughals. Akbar was one of the greatest Mughal emperors. Art and literature received a lot of encouragement under his rule. Several architectural wonders were also built during the Mughal era. The Taj Mahal, one of the Seven Wonders of the World, was built by Akbar's grandson, Shah Jahan.

Further east, Japan witnessed a big change too. It was ruled by an emperor who established a feudal system similar to the one that existed in Europe. The second in command was the shogun, who was the supreme military commander. They were followed by the feudal lords called *daimyo* and knights who were called *samurai*. The peasants and the merchants served the upper class of the society.

Akbar was only 13 years old when he was crowned the King of India.

Machu Picchu is called the Lost City of Incas.
It was primarily used as an observatory, to view stars.

Medieval Americas

Two very important civilisations sprung up in North and South America during the Middle Ages. These were the Aztecs and the Incas. The Aztecs, who lived in Mexico, built huge stone pyramids and made human sacrifices in the temples to please their gods. The Incas lived in South America. Their most famous leader was Pachacuti who expanded his empire to include parts of Chile, Bolivia and Ecuador. Machu Picchu was the most famous city of the Incas.

The Renaissance

The Middle Ages was followed by the Renaissance period. This was a time of great change and development throughout Europe, in the fields of painting, sculpture, literature, science and architecture. Great thinkers and scientists like Nicolaus Copernicus and Galileo studied the universe, while great artists like Leonardo da Vinci, Raphael and Michelangelo created beautiful paintings and sculptures. Michelangelo is famous for paintings such as *The Last Judgment* in the Sistine Chapel and the sculpture *David*.

The statue of David was completed in 1504, after three long years.

Age of Exploration

Man has always longed to learn more about the world around him. This desire has led many explorers to set sail around the globe, discovering not only new lands, but also new religions and cultures.

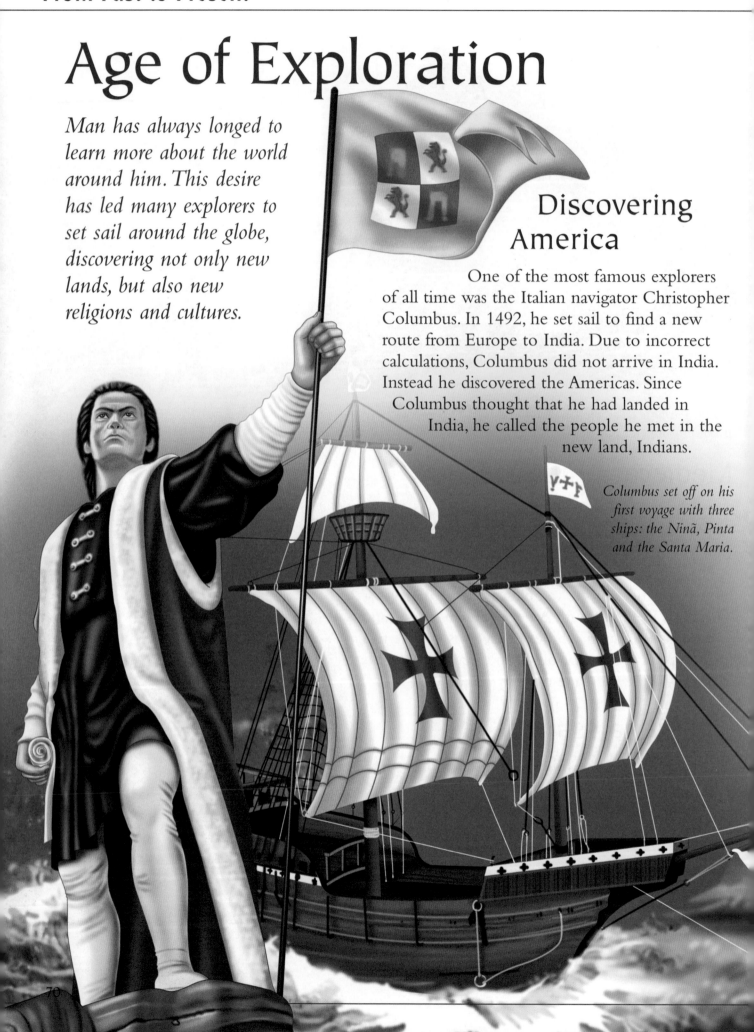

Discovering America

One of the most famous explorers of all time was the Italian navigator Christopher Columbus. In 1492, he set sail to find a new route from Europe to India. Due to incorrect calculations, Columbus did not arrive in India. Instead he discovered the Americas. Since Columbus thought that he had landed in India, he called the people he met in the new land, Indians.

Columbus set off on his first voyage with three ships: the Ninã, Pinta and the Santa Maria.

Exploring Unknown Lands

Vasco da Gama set sail from Portugal in 1497. He sailed around the southern part of Africa and in 1498 became the first European to discover a sea route to India. Britain's Captain James Cook made several trips to discover new lands. In 1768, Cook made his first voyage and landed in New Zealand and Australia. His second voyage began in 1772. This time he discovered a group of islands in the South Pacific that he named the Cook Islands.

Most early explorers depended upon the magnetic compass to find their way across the seas. Today, more advanced navigational tools are used.

James Cook was the first European to set foot on the islands of Hawaii.

The British Empire

Most of the explorations were funded by kings and nobles. One of the main reasons for this was the desire to forge new trade relations. A large part of Europe was under imperial rule during this period. So the European monarchies encouraged their explorers to find new places and promote trade with them. This desire to trade eventually resulted in the colonisation of most of these new countries. Soon empires were set up all over the world.

The British Empire was the biggest empire of all. During the 17th century, Britain set up colonies in North America. Most of these colonies were on the eastern coast. British colonies were also established in the West Indies in 1623. The British soon dominated the slave trade as well. In 1655, the British invaded Jamaica and made it part of their empire. The British set up the East India Company in India in the 17th century to promote trade between the two countries. They later took over the country.

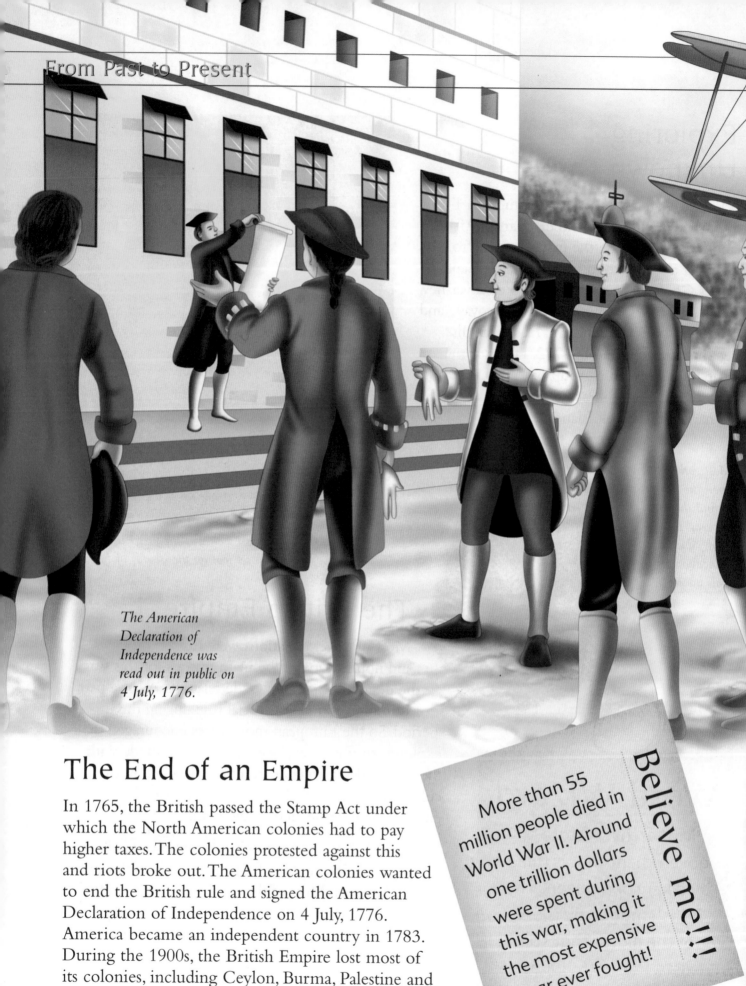

The American Declaration of Independence was read out in public on 4 July, 1776.

The End of an Empire

In 1765, the British passed the Stamp Act under which the North American colonies had to pay higher taxes. The colonies protested against this and riots broke out. The American colonies wanted to end the British rule and signed the American Declaration of Independence on 4 July, 1776. America became an independent country in 1783. During the 1900s, the British Empire lost most of its colonies, including Ceylon, Burma, Palestine and most of the African countries. In 1942, the Quit India movement began in India, which finally gained its independence in 1947.

More than 55 million people died in World War II. Around one trillion dollars were spent during this war, making it the most expensive war ever fought!

Believe me!!!

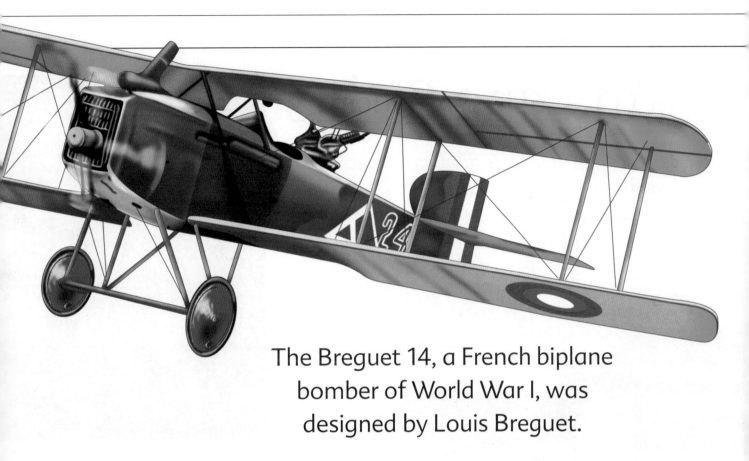

The Breguet 14, a French biplane bomber of World War I, was designed by Louis Breguet.

The World Wars

The First and Second World Wars changed the world in a manner that no other event had before them. The First World War began in August 1914 between the Allied Powers and the Central Powers. The United Kingdom, France, Russia, Italy, Belgium, Serbia, Montenegro and Japan were the Allied Powers. Germany, Austria-Hungary, the Ottoman Empire and Bulgaria formed the Central Powers. One of the main causes of the war was the growing struggle for power. In 1917, the United States also joined the Allies. The war ended on 11 November, 1918 with the Allies emerging as the victors. More than 10 million people were killed in this war.

The Second World War was fought between the Allies and the Axis powers. Germany, Italy and Japan were the three main countries that formed the Axis powers and Britain, France, USSR and USA were the Allies. The war began on 1 September, 1939, when Germany, under Adolph Hitler, attacked Poland. The war ended in September 1945. The Second World War is remembered for the huge amount of destruction and some very cruel incidents. One of these was the dropping of the atomic bomb on two Japanese cities, Hiroshima and Nagasaki.

Adolph Hitler was responsible for the Holocaust, a period where over six million Jews were killed.

Amazing Sights

The world around us is filled with some remarkable wonders. Some are man-made and some are natural. A few of the amazing sights that one should not miss are shown below.

Over 10 million tourists visit Niagara Falls every year!

There are seven points, or rays, in the crown of the Statue of Liberty. These rays represent the seven seas and the continents of the world.

Wonders of the World

Niagara Falls are found in North America on the Niagara River. The waterfalls were formed around 12,000 years ago and have two parts – the Horseshoe Falls that fall in Canada and the American Falls in the United States.

The **Statue of Liberty** is located in New York. It shows a woman holding a flame in her right hand and a tablet in her left hand. The tablet has the date 'July 4, 1776' written on it, which is the Independence Day of the United States. The statue is 92 metres high and was built in Paris. It was a gift from France to the USA.

The **Grand Canyon** is found in Arizona, USA. It is more than 1,524 metres deep, and is 446 kilometres long and almost

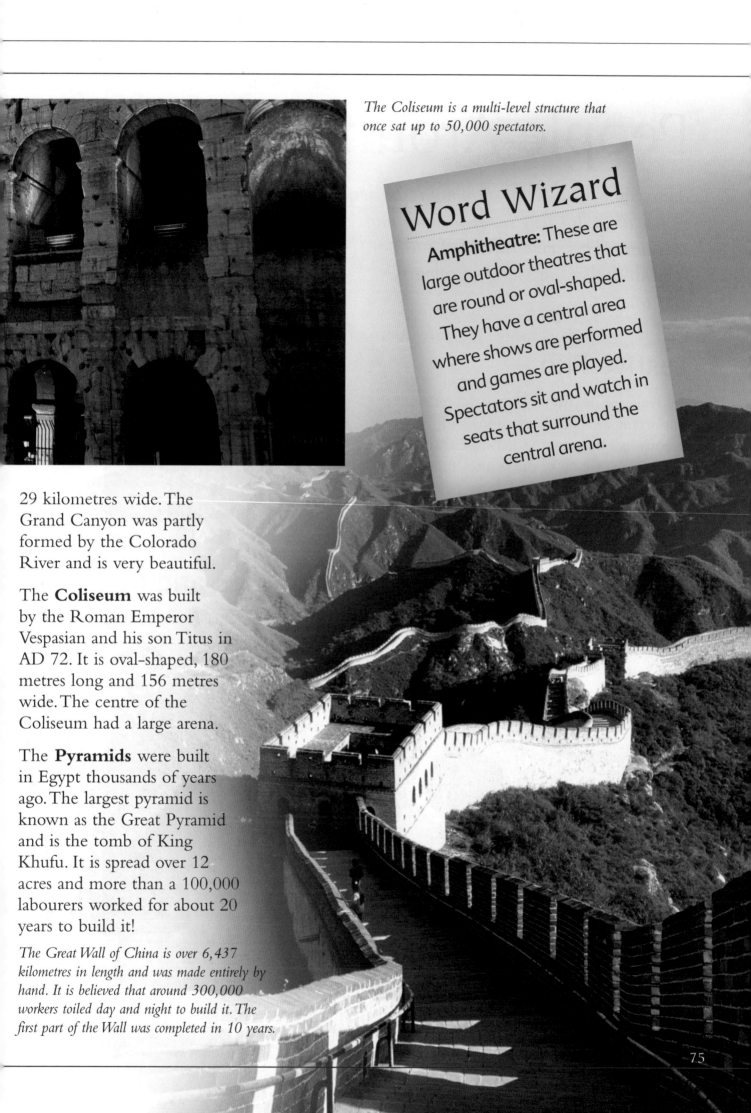

The Coliseum is a multi-level structure that once sat up to 50,000 spectators.

Word Wizard

Amphitheatre: These are large outdoor theatres that are round or oval-shaped. They have a central area where shows are performed and games are played. Spectators sit and watch in seats that surround the central arena.

29 kilometres wide. The Grand Canyon was partly formed by the Colorado River and is very beautiful.

The **Coliseum** was built by the Roman Emperor Vespasian and his son Titus in AD 72. It is oval-shaped, 180 metres long and 156 metres wide. The centre of the Coliseum had a large arena.

The **Pyramids** were built in Egypt thousands of years ago. The largest pyramid is known as the Great Pyramid and is the tomb of King Khufu. It is spread over 12 acres and more than a 100,000 labourers worked for about 20 years to build it!

The Great Wall of China is over 6,437 kilometres in length and was made entirely by hand. It is believed that around 300,000 workers toiled day and night to build it. The first part of the Wall was completed in 10 years.

People Around Us

The world is made up of many countries, each with a different set of customs and traditions. This wide variety of cultures is what makes our world so colourful and interesting.

Festive Fun

Festivals are usually held to celebrate important or special occasions and events. In Hungary, the Buso Festival is held to scare away the winter months and welcome spring. In China, people celebrate the Chinese Lantern Festival.

Hallowe'en was once known as 'mischief night' in England.

Food Fiesta

Burgers, fish and chips or sushi – nearly every country is identified with a special kind of food. Some European countries like France, Holland and Denmark are known for their cheese and wine, while Italy is the home of pizza and pasta.

Countries and Costumes

There are many styles of dressing across the globe. The Indian sari and the German lederhosen (short leather trousers) are amongst well-known national costumes. The kimono is worn in Japan on special occasions. It is a full-length, wraparound garment. In the British Isles, one of the best known costumes is the Scottish kilt, with its tartan pattern.

Sushi is one of the most famous Japanese delicacies.

Index

Index